To Zona,
It only takes one person.
Anna Housel Hamilton

The Poor Little Slave Girl

Anna Housel Hamilton

Copyright © 2011 Anna Housel Hamilton.

All rights reserved. No part of this book may be used or reproduced by any means, graphic, electronic, or mechanical, including photocopying, recording, taping or by any information storage retrieval system without the written permission of the publisher except in the case of brief quotations embodied in critical articles and reviews.

ISBN: 978-1-4497-2338-5 (sc)
Library of Congress Control Number: 2011913898

WestBow Press books may be ordered through booksellers or by contacting:

WestBow Press
A Division of Thomas Nelson
1663 Liberty Drive
Bloomington, IN 47403
www.westbowpress.com
1-(866) 928-1240

Because of the dynamic nature of the Internet, any web addresses or links contained in this book may have changed since publication and may no longer be valid. The views expressed in this work are solely those of the author and do not necessarily reflect the views of the publisher, and the publisher hereby disclaims any responsibility for them.

Any people depicted in stock imagery provided by Thinkstock are models, and such images are being used for illustrative purposes only.

Certain stock imagery © Thinkstock.

Printed in the United States of America

WestBow Press rev. date: 8/18/2011

"An unusually blessed book. You will be personally affected by the message."
Henry T. Blackaby

Henry T. Blackaby is the president of Henry Blackaby Ministries. He is a popular speaker and writer whose study course ***Experiencing God*** has sold more than 3,000,000 copies.

What can a poor little slave girl do for God?
This is an amazing story of bravery and faith of a little, nameless girl.

Who does God use to send a message? Whoever is available and willing to obey Him! In this case He used a humble, obedient, insignificant, person to show that there was a real God available to answer prayers! This story is taken from the Bible: II Kings 5: 1-19 - I was inspired to write the story for a first and second grade Sunday School Class that I taught. I used clip art in the original book, and was encouraged by friends to paint the illustrations and publish the book for you to enjoy.

ACKNOWLEDGEMENTS:

I would like to thank my granddaughter, Destiny Worthy, for being the model as the little Slave Girl in this book. I would also like to thank the following people, as without them this book would not have happened: My husband, Lloyd, my friends, Beverly & Nathan Ensley, Linda Pollok, Miller Collum, Gary Suwinski, Greg Lee, Brandan Caruso, and my grandson, Chris Worthy. God has blessed me with His very best!

Naaman was the commander in chief of the king's army. He was an important man.

The king liked Naaman, because he had a strong army. One day lots of Naaman's soldiers invaded a city in Israel and took people as slaves. Among those taken was a little girl.

We don't know her name, or even how old she was. We do know that she lost everything, except her faith in God.

She was given to Naaman's wife as a servant.

How do you think you would feel if soldiers kidnapped you from your home and you had to be a slave to someone?

A slave has to work hard and do what they are told to do. The little girl was in a hopeless situation! She had plenty of reasons to have a bad attitude. However, when she found out that Naaman had leprosy, she felt sorry for him! She knew what God could do! Perhaps her parents told her the story of Joseph. Joseph was a slave at one time too. We know the wonderful story about how God took care of him and he later saved his whole family from starvation. Maybe that's why she had such a good attitude. She lost her family, but not her faith in God!

We do know that the little girl knew that if Elisha prayed to his God, Naaman would be healed. However, if she spoke out of turn, she may be punished. People might laugh if she told them about Elisha. What do you think the little girl did? You know what? That brave little girl went to Naaman's wife and told her that there was a man of God in Israel that could help Naaman. She said: "If only my master would see the prophet who is in Samaria! He would cure him of his leprosy." II Kings 5:3 NIV Naaman went to the king of Aram. The king said he would help Naaman. He gave him $20,000 in silver, $60.000. in gold and ten suites of clothing. He also wrote a letter to the king of Israel to ask him to help Naaman.

When Naaman gave the letter to the king of Israel the king was very upset! He knew he couldn't heal Naaman. He thought maybe Naaman would invade his country again! Oh, he was worried! Everyone in Israel must have been talking about the king's problem.

Everyone in Israel must have known that Naaman's army visited the king! When Elisha heard about the king's problem he sent a message to the king.

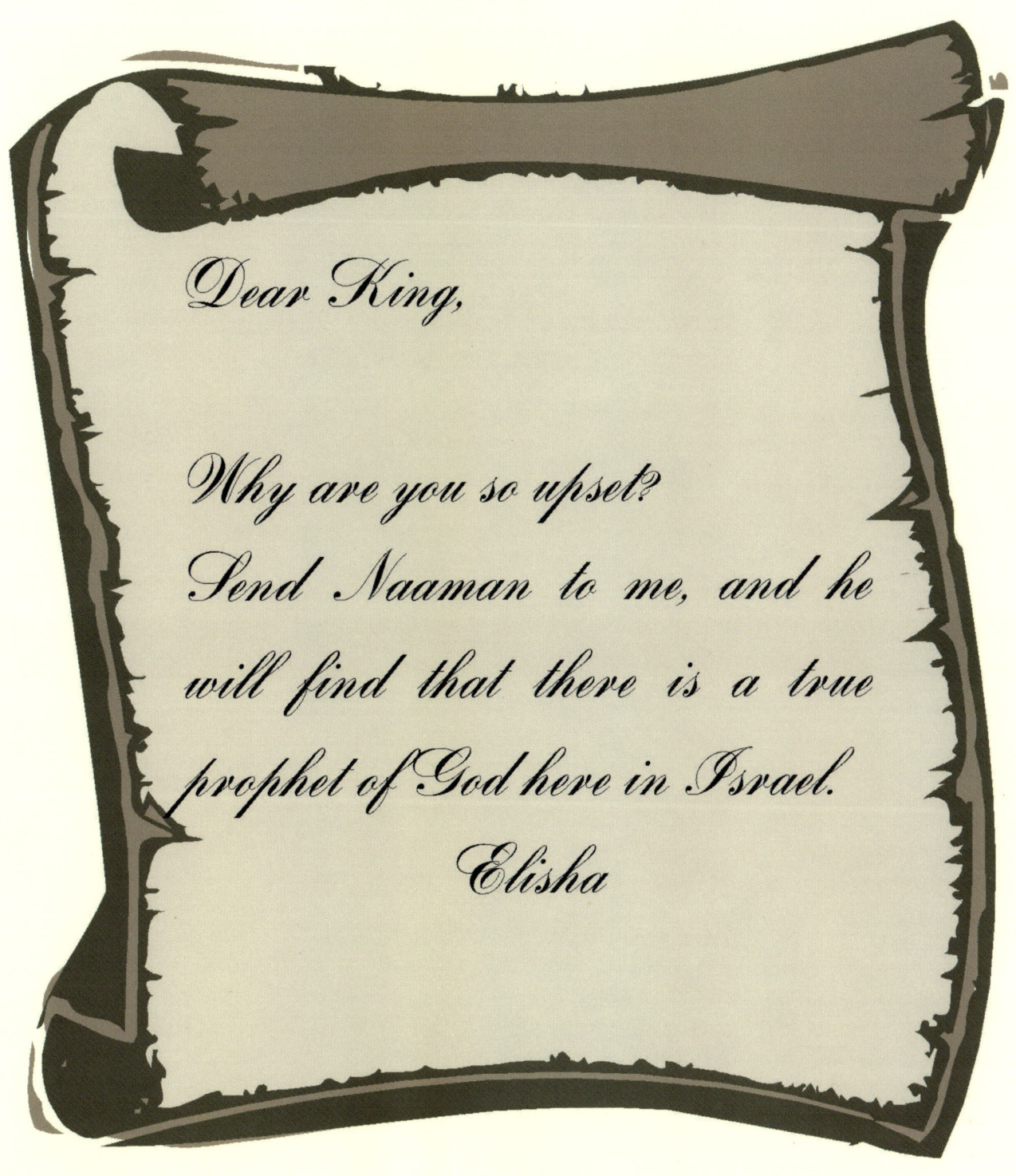

Dear King,

Why are you so upset? Send Naaman to me, and he will find that there is a true prophet of God here in Israel.

Elisha

Imagine this: Here comes Naaman with his horses and army! Do you think Elisha ran to the door? You will never Are they going to have dinner? No! Elisha sent a messenger Jordan River and wash seven times and then he would be

chariots. He stood at the door of Elisha's home with his
guess what Elisha did. Will Naaman be invited in for tea?
to the door! The messenger told Naaman to go to the
healed of the leprosy!

Naaman got angry! He must have thought that Elisha was playing a joke on him. Wash seven times! He said: "Look, I thought at least he would come out and talk to me! I expected him to wave his hand over the leprosy and call upon the name of his God, and I would be healed."

Oh, he was upset alright! Then he said "If it's the river I need I'll wash at home and get rid of my leprosy!" He had clean rivers in the land of Aram. The Jordan river was not the prettiest river to look at! He was so angry he stalked away!

Then one of the officers asked him if Elisha would have had him do a great thing, would he do it? After all, they did make the trip to see the man of God. Naaman really did want to get rid of the leprosy. Maybe Elisha's God could help him. This was a simple thing to do.

We really don't know everything the officer said to Naaman. But then, after thinking about it for a while, Naaman decided to obey the man that prayed to the one true God!

So he went to the river and washed one, two, three, four, five, six, and then seven times!

The leprosy was gone! The Bible tells us his skin was like a child's. Wow! He and his entire army went back to find Elisha! They were so happy! Naaman told Elisha that he would only worship the one true God.

If the little servant girl would not have been kind and told Naaman's wife about Elisha, many people would not have heard about the one true God! We are still talking about this story thousands of years later!

In Luke 4:27 the Bible tells us that there were many lepers in Israel in the time of Elisha. Naaman was the only one healed.

It only takes one person to tell another person about the love of our God.

Imagine how happy they all were when Naaman and the army returned home! I bet they all had a party and celebrated with the little girl. Sadly, she's not mentioned again. Oh, I hope we see them in heaven, so that we can talk to them about that wonderful day! Because of the love of one little girl, Naaman, his wife, his family, and his army, all learned about the wonderful God that we worship!

CPSIA information can be obtained
at www.ICGtesting.com
Printed in the USA
243682LV00002B